Mountain Lions

Mountain Lions

Maura Gouck

THE CHILD'S WORLD®, INC.

Published in the United States of America by The Child's World®, Inc.
PO Box 326
Chanhassen, MN 55317-0326
800-599-READ
www.childsworld.com

Product Manager Mary Berendes
Editor Katherine Stevenson
Designer Mary Berendes
Contributor Bob Temple

Photo Credits
© 1991 Alan G. Nelson/Dembinsky Photo Assoc. Inc.: 10
© 2001 Chuck Pefley/Stone: 13
© Daniel J. Cox/naturalexposures.com: cover, 6, 15, 16, 19, 20, 23, 26
© 1994 Dominique Braud/Dembinsky Photo Assoc. Inc.: 29
© 1998 Jim Roetzel/Dembinsky Photo Assoc. Inc.: 2
© Joe McDonald/www.hoothollow.com: 9
© 1994 Mark J. Thomas/Dembinsky Photo Assoc. Inc.: 30
© 2001 Tom Tietz/Stone: 24

Library of Congress Cataloging-in-Publication Data
Gouck, Maura.
Mountain lions / by Maura Gouck.
p. cm.
Includes index.
ISBN 1-56766-888-7 (library bound : alk. paper)
1. Puma—Juvenile literature. [1. Puma.] I. Title.
QL737.C23 G67 2001
599.75'24—dc21
00-010773

On the cover...

Front cover: This adult is watching the photographer during a snowstorm in Montana.
Page 2: From close up, it's easy to see how beautiful this mountain lion is.

Table of Contents

Chapter	Page
Meet the Mountain Lion!	7
What Are Mountain Lions?	8
What Do Mountain Lions Look Like?	11
Where Do Mountain Lions Live?	12
Do Mountain Lions Live Alone?	14
What Are Baby Mountain Lions Like?	17
What Do Mountain Lions Eat?	18
How Do Mountain Lions Hunt?	21
How Do Mountain Lions Eat?	25
Do Mountain Lions Have Enemies?	27
Glossary, Index, & Web Sites	32

In a snowy forest, a deer nibbles on some plants. It picks up its head, listening for signs of danger. The deer doesn't know that it is being watched. Nearby, another creature sits quietly, its long tail swaying back and forth. Suddenly, the creature leaps toward the deer. After a short chase, it clamps its jaws around the deer's neck, then drags the deer to a hidden place for dinner. What is this silent attacker? It's a mountain lion!

What Are Mountain Lions?

Mountain lions belong to a group of animals called **mammals.** Mammals have hair or fur and feed their babies milk from their bodies. Dogs, cats, cows, and people are mammals, too.

Mountain lions got their name because they look like the female lions that live in Africa. Even though they look alike, the cats are two different types, or **species,** of lion. Mountain lions are sometimes called *cougars* or *pumas.*

From close up, it's easy to see how much ⇒ mountain lions look like the lions of Africa.

What Do Mountain Lions Look Like?

Mountain lions are smaller than African lions, but they are still big cats with powerful bodies. A full-grown male can be eight feet long and can weigh up to 200 pounds! Unlike lions and tigers, mountain lions can't roar. Instead, they make sounds such as hissing and growling.

Mountain lions have round faces with small, round ears. They also have long tails—unlike short-tailed wild cats such as lynxes and bobcats. Their thick fur can be reddish brown or gray, depending on where they live. Brown mountain lions often live in warmer areas. Gray mountain lions live in colder areas.

⇐ This adult has climbed a tree stump to take a better look around.

Where Do Mountain Lions Live?

From the sound of their name, you would think mountain lions lived only in rugged, snow-covered mountains. But that's not the case. They live in many different parts of North and South America. Mountain lions can make themselves at home in almost any area and almost any type of weather. They have been found in cold, snowy regions of Canada and high in the mountain forests of Washington and California. They even live in the warm, tropical forests of Central and South America.

This mountain lion is standing on a snowy peak in Montana. ⇒

Do Mountain Lions Live Alone?

Each mountain lion lives alone within a home area, or **territory.** There it hunts, sleeps, and raises its babies. You've probably seen a cat sharpening its claws on a living-room chair. Mountain lions do the same thing—but they use a tree! Mountain lions scratch trees and leave body scents to mark their territories. If a mountain lion sees scratch marks and smells another cat's scent, it knows that territory has already been claimed.

This adult is leaving scratch marks on a dead tree. ⇒

What Are Baby Mountain Lions Like?

Like house cats, mountain lions begin life as tiny **cubs.** A female mountain lion usually has two to four cubs at a time. The cubs weigh only about one pound at birth. They are born blind but can see in about ten days.

Baby mountain lions don't look much like their mothers. They are covered with large dark spots, and their short tails have dark rings. The cubs stay with their mother for almost two years, until they can hunt on their own.

⇐ This young cub is exploring in the green grass of a Montana forest.

What Do Mountain Lions Eat?

Like other cats, mountain lions are **carnivores,** or meat-eaters. Their favorite food animals, or **prey,** are large animals such as deer and elk. If they can't find these animals, they settle for smaller prey such as rabbits, beavers, or squirrels.

This mountain lion is trying to catch a porcupine ⇒ that has climbed a tree to escape.

How Do Mountain Lions Hunt?

Mountain lions hunt alone, usually at night. Their eyes see well at night, and their whiskers help them feel their way in the dark.

Mountain lions can run very fast, but they tire quickly. They **stalk,** or sneak up on, their prey so they do not have to chase it very far. Their paws are padded so they can move quietly. They crouch down close to the ground, hiding behind branches or grass whenever they can.

⇐ This adult mountain lion is stalking a herd of mule deer in the Rocky Mountains.

Once the mountain lion is close enough, it leaps out and rushes toward its prey. As the cat runs, its toes spread apart and its claws come out. The claws are very sharp, and the mountain lion uses them to catch and hold its prey. Then the cat clamps its powerful jaws around the victim's neck. Unable to breathe, the prey animal soon dies, and the mountain lion enjoys its meal.

This large adult has killed a bighorn sheep in southern Utah. ⇒

A mountain lion's mouth is well designed for eating meat. It opens wide and has big front teeth that help the cat kill its prey. The teeth along the sides of its mouth are sharp and pointed—perfect for tearing off pieces of meat. Mountain lions don't chew their food. Instead, they swallow it in large chunks.

A mountain lion also uses its tongue as another tool for eating. If a house cat has ever licked you, you know that its tongue feels like fine sandpaper. The roughness you feel is actually many tiny hooks! A mountain lion's tongue is the same, only larger. The mountain lion uses its rough tongue to clean meat off the bones of its prey.

⇐ Here you can see this mountain lion's teeth and tongue as it hisses at the photographer.

Do Mountain Lions Have Enemies?

In some areas the mountain lion is known as the "ghost cat." People see its pawprints and find the remains of its dinner, but they rarely see the cat itself. Mountain lions have made themselves hard to find for a good reason! People are this cat's greatest enemy. Farmers and ranchers think mountain lions are a nuisance because they occasionally attack herds of sheep or cows. Some people shoot, trap, and poison the cats to keep them away.

⇐ Mountain lions are skilled jumpers. A high gap is no problem for this Utah mountain lion.

Despite what many people think, mountain lions are not our enemies. These cats rarely injure people, and they are not a great threat to ranchers. Mountain lions prefer to hunt weak, sick, or old animals. Actually, they help farmers by killing animals such as deer that eat the farmers' crops.

This mountain lion is curious about ⇒
something it saw moving in the grass.

Mountain lions are now protected in some areas where they are rare. In areas where they are more common, laws help control when and how people can hunt them. Scientists are studying ways for mountain lions and people to live in the same regions without interfering with each other. Like so many other animals, mountain lions can survive if we learn how to share our space with them.

Glossary

carnivores (KAR-nih-vorz)
Carnivores are animals that kill and eat other animals for food.
Mountain lions are carnivores.

cubs (KUBZ)
Baby mountain lions are called cubs. Mountain lions usually
have two to four cubs at a time.

mammals (MAM-mullz)
Mammals are animals that are warm-blooded, have hair on their
bodies, and feed their babies milk from their bodies. Mountain
lions are mammals, and so are people.

prey (PRAY)
Prey animals are those that are hunted and killed for food.
Mountain lions hunt large prey, such as deer and elk.

species (SPEE-sheez)
A species is a different kind or type of an animal. Mountain
lions and African lions are two different species.

stalk (STAWK)
To stalk something is to quietly follow or sneak up on it.
Mountain lions hunt animals by stalking them.

territory (TEHR-ih-tor-ee)
A territory is an area of land that an animal claims as its own.
Each mountain lion has a territory it guards against intruders.

Web Sites

http://www.mountainlion.org/

http://www.primenet.com/~brendel/puma.html

http://home.iprimus.com.au/tigris/mount_lion.htm

Index

appearance, 8

carnivores, 18

claws, 14, 22

cubs, 17

eating, 25

enemies, 27

hunting habits, 7, 21

location, 12, 14, 27

mammals, 8

other names for, 8

prey, 18, 21, 22, 25

protection of, 31

sounds, 11

species, 8

territory, 14

tongue, 25